Pocahontas

by Lucia Raatma

Compass Point Early Biographies

*Content Adviser: Professor Sherry L. Field,
Department of Social Science Education, College of Education,
The University of Georgia*

*Reading Adviser: Dr. Linda D. Labbo,
Department of Reading Education, College of Education,
The University of Georgia*

COMPASS POINT BOOKS

Minneapolis, Minnesota

Compass Point Books
3722 West 50th Street, #115
Minneapolis, MN 55410

Visit Compass Point Books on the Internet at *www.compasspointbooks.com* or e-mail your
request to *custserv@compasspointbooks.com*

Editors: E. Russell Primm, Emily J. Dolbear, and Laura Driscoll
Photo Researcher: Svetlana Zhurkina
Photo Selector: Linda S. Koutris
Designer: Bradfordesign, Inc.

Library of Congress Cataloging-in-Publication Data

Raatma, Lucia.
    Pocahontas / by Lucia Raatma.
        p. cm. — (Compass Point early biographies)
    Includes bibliographical references and index.
    ISBN 0-7565-0115-6 (hardcover : lib. bdg.)
        1. Pocahontas, 1595?–1617—Juvenile literature. 2. Powhatan women—Biography—Juvenile liter-
ature. [1. Pocahontas, 1595?–1617. 2. Powhatan Indians. 3. Women—Biography.] I. Title. II. Series.
    E99.P85 P5757 2002
    975.5'02'092—dc21   2001001579

Table of Contents

A Playful Little Girl

Pocahontas was the daughter of a Native American chief. She helped the English **settlers** who came to live in America. She was an important person in early American history.

A Native American village

Pocahontas was born around 1595, before the United States became a country. She lived in an area that is now called Virginia.

Her father, Powhatan, was a great Indian chief. He ruled thirty tribes.

Pocahontas helped the early settlers.

Pocahontas's real name was Matoaka. Only members of her tribe called her by that name. *Pocahontas*, her nickname, meant "playful little girl." She loved to play in the woods near her village.

Pocahontas lived in what is now known as Virginia.

Men from England

When Pocahontas was about twelve years old, her life changed. Men from England came from across the sea. They built a settlement called Jamestown. It was near Pocahontas's village.

These men looked different from Pocahontas and her people. Their clothes were different.

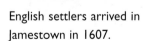

English settlers arrived in Jamestown in 1607.

Their language was different. They carried guns. Captain John Smith was the leader of these

Captain John Smith

Englishmen. One day, hunters from one of Powhatan's tribes took John Smith from Jamestown. They brought him to Chief Powhatan.

Years later, John Smith wrote that Powhatan had wanted to kill him.

8

He said that Pocahontas saved his life. This may or may not be true.

It is true that Pocahontas helped John Smith, though. She helped him get along with her father.

Soon, the Indians began to trade with the English. They traded food and furs for weapons and tools.

The English traded with the Native Americans.

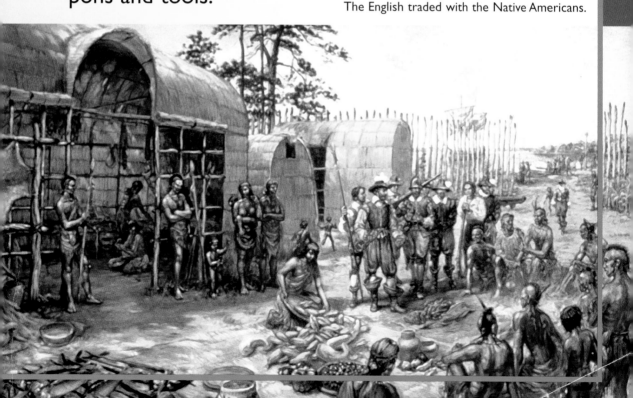

Keeping the Peace

For a few years, Pocahontas helped to keep peace between the English settlers and her people. The English did not have enough food. Pocahontas brought food to Jamestown. She kept the English from **starving**.

Pocahontas always looked for John Smith when she visited James-town. She liked him very much. She felt they were good friends.

In the early years, the people of Jamestown had very little food.

Ships brought more settlers and more food to Jamestown.

More and more English settlers arrived in Jamestown. Women and children joined the men. The English liked the rich soil of Virginia. They began to take over the area.

The Indians had lived there for hundreds of years. The English did not accept that the land belonged to Powhatan's people. The Native Americans began to dislike the English. Fighting often broke out between the two groups.

The settlers and the Native Americans fought over land.

Losing a Friend

In 1609, John Smith was hurt in an **accident**. He was put on a boat and sent back to England.

The next time Pocahontas visited Jamestown, the settlers told her John Smith was dead. She was very sad. She felt she had lost a good friend.

A statue of John Smith at Jamestown ➤

Taken from the Tribe

Over time, the Native Americans and the English fought more and more. Powhatan did not trust the settlers now. He stopped helping them.

In 1613, the English took Pocahontas from her people. They told Powhatan they would return his daughter if he gave them corn and other goods.

Powhatan was a proud man. He sent only some of the things the English wanted. He asked them to treat his daughter well, but he did not try to save her.

Chief Powhatan

The English took Pocahontas ▶
away from her people.

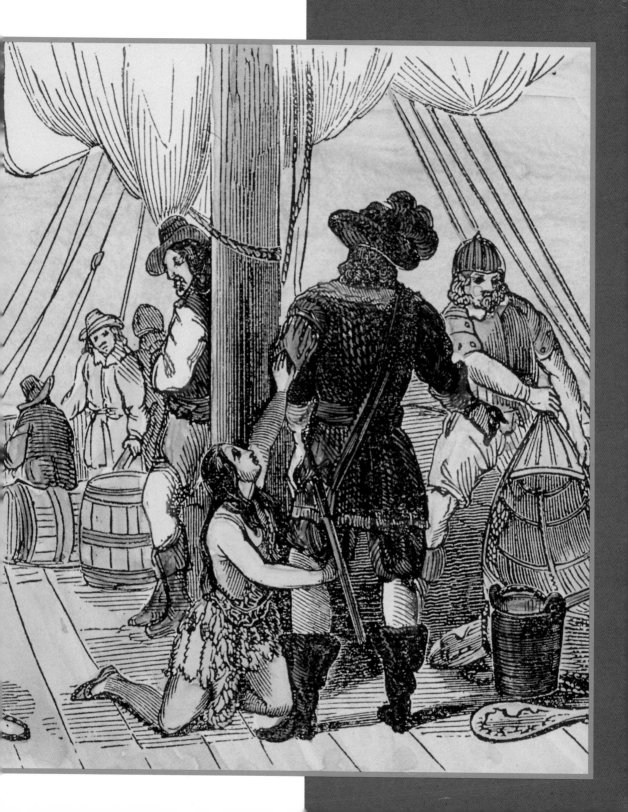

English Ways

For almost a year, Pocahontas lived with the English settlers. They made her dress like they

Pocahontas in English clothes

did. She wore long dresses with high necks. She wore tight shoes. She put her hair up with hairpins.

The English also taught Pocahontas about their god. They were **Christians**. They did not agree with the beliefs of the Indians.

Pocahontas became a Christian. ➤

John Rolfe

The English told Pocahontas to forget what she had learned as a child. Little by little, she followed the English ways.

Soon Pocahontas met John Rolfe, another English settler. His wife and daughter had died, so he was also alone.

John Rolfe liked Pocahontas. He taught her about being a Christian and spent a lot of time with her. Soon John Rolfe fell in love with Pocahontas.

A New Family

Pocahontas became a Christian. She learned how to act like an Englishwoman too. The English gave her a new name. They called her "Rebecca." In 1614, she and John Rolfe decided to marry.

When Powhatan heard that his daughter was going to marry John Rolfe, he thought it was a good idea. He felt the marriage would

Pocahontas and her son, Thomas

bring peace between the English and the Indians. He was right. For a few years, there was peace.

Pocahontas and John Rolfe had a son around 1615. They named him Thomas.

Soon the family traveled to London, England. The other settlers thought the king of England would like to meet Pocahontas.

The wedding of Pocahontas and John Rolfe

In England

Pocahontas met many people in England. She went to parties and met the king and queen. London was a large and busy city. Pocahontas did not like the crowds or the noise.

She was happier when she and her family left London. They lived in a country house outside the city.

In London, Pocahontas met the king and queen.

London at about the time Pocahontas moved there

Then Pocahontas got a big surprise. She found out that John Smith was still alive! She wanted to see him. But for months, he did not come to visit her.

A TRVE RElation of fuch occurrences and accidents of noateas hath hapned in Virginia fince the firft planting ofthat Collony, which is now refident in the South part thereof, till the laft returne from thence.

Written by Captaine Smith *one of the faid Collony, to a worfhipfull* friend of his in England.

LONDON

Printed for *Iohn Tappe*, and are to bee folde at the Greyhound in Paules-Church-yard by *W.W.*
1608

John Smith wrote this book about his adventures in Virginia.

When John Smith finally came, Pocahontas was angry. She had thought they were friends. She had done so much to help him and the other settlers. But some say John Smith was not **sincere**.

He pretended to be Pocahontas's friend in order to get things from her father.

Even so, Pocahontas told John Smith that they would always be special friends. After that day, however, they never saw each other again.

The cold English weather was hard on Pocahontas. She began to feel sick. She may have come down with an illness that hurt her lungs.

John Rolfe decided it was time to go back to Virginia. Pocahontas did not want to go back. She knew that the English and the Indians could not get along. She wanted to stay away from the fighting.

A Short Life

John Rolfe planned their trip anyway. In March 1617, he boarded a ship with Pocahontas and Thomas. They set sail for Virginia.

Soon Pocahontas knew she was too sick to go on. She asked to be taken ashore near

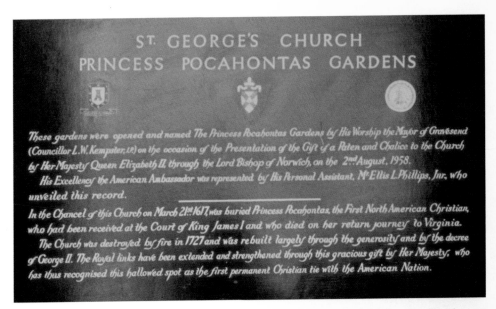

A sign at Gravesend, England, honors Pocahontas.

Gravesend, England

Gravesend, England. That is where she died. She was only about twenty-two years old.

John Rolfe went the rest of the way to Virginia where he later died. Young Thomas grew up in England with other members of his family.

Pocahontas lived a short life. But her life was important. She helped keep the peace between the English and the Native Americans. She gave food to the settlers and helped them **survive** in their new home.

It was sad that the English took the land from her people. They also made Pocahontas into someone she was not.

If Pocahontas had not helped the first English settlers, they might have died. Then Jamestown might not have lasted. The United States might never have become the country it is today.

◀ A statue of Pocahontas at Jamestown

Important Dates in Pocahontas's Life

1595	Born in or about this year
1607	English settlers establish the settlement of Jamestown
1609	John Smith is hurt and returns to England
1610– 1612	Jamestown struggles to survive
1613	Is taken from her tribe by the English
1614	Marries John Rolfe
1615	Pocahontas gives birth to a son, Thomas, at about this time
1616	Travels to England with John Rolfe and Thomas
1617	Dies near Gravesend, England

Glossary

accident—an event that is not expected and often includes injuries

Christians—people who believe Jesus Christ is the son of God

settlers—people who make a home in a new place

sincere—honest and truthful

starving—dying from hunger

survive—to stay alive

Did You Know?

- After he grew up, Pocahontas's son, Thomas, went back to Virginia to live.

- Today, many people in the United States claim to be related to Pocahontas and John Rolfe.

- Jamestown was the first successful English settlement in America.

- The site of the Jamestown settlement is now a museum in the state of Virginia.

Want to Know More?

At the Library

Covert, Kim. *The Powhatan People*. Mankato, Minn.: Bridgestone Books, 1999.

Jenner, Caryn. *The Story of Pocahontas*. New York: DK Publishing, 2000.

Milton, Joyce. *Pocahontas: An American Princess*. New York: Grosset & Dunlap, 2000.

Vann, Edith. *Pocahontas*. Austin, Tex.: Raintree Steck-Vaughn, 1995.

On the Web

Four Faces of Pocahontas

http://www.co.henrico.va.us/manager/pokeypix.htm

For a biography of Pocahontas and four portraits of the Native American princess

The Real Pocahontas

http://www.geocities.com/Broadway/1001/poca_main.html

For a discussion of how the real story of Pocahontas differs from the animated film

Through the Mail

Association for the Preservation of Virginia Antiquities:
Jamestown Rediscovery

1367 Colonial Parkway

Jamestown, VA 23081

To get information on recent discoveries at Jamestown

On the Road

Jamestown Settlement

Route 31 South at the Colonial Parkway

Jamestown, VA 23081

888/593-4682

To see recreations of a Jamestown fort, a Native American village, and the settlers' ships

Index

About the Author
Lucia Raatma received her bachelor's degree in English literature from the University of South Carolina and her master's degree in cinema studies from New York University.
She has written a wide range of books for young people. When she is not researching or writing, she enjoys going to movies, playing tennis, and spending time with her husband, daughter, and golden retriever. She lives in New York.

Ø
1/02
10. 6/05